Who Are You?
By Jacqueline James
Published by Parables
December 2021   All Rights Reserved.
No part of this book may be reproduced or utilized in any form or by any means, electronic or mechanical, including photocopying, recording, or by any information storage and retrieval system, without the permission in writing from the author.
ISBN 978-1-954308-78-7 Copyright by Jacqueline James

Who are you?

Written by Jacqueline James

Illustrated by Davonne Newell

Roses are Red

Violets are Blue

I am a

POETESS

Who are you?

I am a

RACER

running fast,
I will come
in first
and not in last.

I am a
PILOT
flying high,
In a giant
airplane
above the sky.

I am a
DANCER
full of grace,
Admire the poise
on my face.

I am a DOCTOR

I am medically smart,
I can prolong life when I do my part.

I am a
MAIL CARRIER
I deliver mail,
With important messages,
some written in braille.

I am a
SEAMSTRESS
I make clothes,
I help people to look nice
from their head to their toes.

I am a
BAKER
who makes cakes and pies, Making pastries tasty before your eyes.

I am a
TEACHER
I teach at school,
I help students
learn life rules.

I am an
ATHLETE
I play sports,
I compete
with all
my heart.

I am a
JUDGE
I work in a court,
I handle
the law with
legal support.

I am a FIREFIGHTER I put out fires, I save lives when its required.

I am a **SAILOR** sailing the sea, to the many adventures waiting on me.

I am a
POLICE
OFFICER
I stop crimes,
I keep people safe
most of the time.

I am a HOMEMAKER

I stay at home,
Taking care
of my family
all day long.

I am a CUSTODIAN

I clean the floors, I sweep and mop and a whole lot more.

I am an
EXECUTIVE
I make decisions,
I work
in the office with
limited
restrictions.

I am a
SANITATION WORKER
I drive a big truck,
I dispose waste and clean things up.

I am a **LIFEGUARD** I work at a swimming pool, I prevent people from drowning morning, nights and afternoons.

I am a ZOOKEEPER

I take care of animals from all over the globe, so viewers can study their lives as they unfold.

I am an
ASTRONAUT
I travel through space,
from different time zones with many obstacles to face.

I am a
FARMER
I tend the land,
Planting fruits
and vegetables
for life demands.

I am a VOCALIST

I sing songs, Changing melodies as the rhythm goes on.

I am a SERVER

I bring customers their meals, Nutritious and delicious to seal the deal.

I am a CARPENTER

I build beautiful homes, In order to purchase one you may need a loan.

I am a LABORER

I work on an assembly line, Making widgets one of a kind.

I am a
DRIVER

I chauffeur people around, To several destinations around the town.

I am an
ARTIST
I draw
and I paint,
My exquisite
talent is
quite a sight.

I am a
DENTIST
I take care of your teeth, I keep them healthy so you can chew the food you eat.

I am a **PLUMBER** sometimes my job gets dirty, I unclog your pipes so you don't worry.

I am a
METEOROLOGIST
I predict the weather,
I help people dress appropriate for their gatherings.

I am a
JEWELER

I sell sparkling things,

From necklaces and pendants to wedding rings.

I fix computers,
I am a
TECHNICIAN
I earn a generous salary from my position.

I'm a
CLERGYMAN
I work in a church
I give the members a spiritual burst.

I'm the **PRESIDENT** of the United States I keep the country running in its proper place.

Roses are Red
Violets are Blue
I am
IMPORTANT
and so are
YOU!

About the Author

Author Jacqueline James is a brilliant writer with a 5-Star rating, who specializes in poetry and children's stories.
Jacqueline has been gifted to convert challenging situations to unlimited possibilities with her creative writer skills. She brings encouragement as well as joyful moments when exploring the essence of her work.

If you would like to read other books written by Jacqueline James, please visit her website at rhymes64.weebly.com

Davonne is a 14-year-old, self-taught young illustrator with hopes of becoming a successful commission artist. She is very passionate about diversity and inclusion and expresses that passion in the characters she has created for this book. Davonne enjoys creating both digital and traditional style art, and enjoys drawing anime and horror themed art. She also does custom cartooning and chose to use a cartoon that she created of herself to showcase her talent in this area.

If you would like to see more of her work, please visit her instagram at dweeby.creates@IG.com.

www.ingramcontent.com/pod-product-compliance
Lightning Source LLC
Chambersburg PA
CBHW080014090526
44578CB00013B/766